CONTEM

WHEN GOD HIDES

Joseph Evans

© 2025 SLG Press
First Edition 2025

Contemplative Poetry 16

ISBN 978-0-7283-0416-1
Contemplative Poetry Series ISBN 978-0-7283-0319-5

Joseph Evans asserts his right under the Copyright, Designs and Patents Act 1988, to be identified as the author of this work.

All rights reserved. No part of this publication may be reproduced, stored in a retrieval system, or transmitted in any form or by any means, electronic, mechanical, photocopying, recording or otherwise, without the prior written permission of the copyright holder.

Imprimatur
+ Rt. Rev. Philip A. Egan BA, STL, PhD
Bishop of Portsmouth
6 February 2025

Edited, designed and typeset in Bembo by Julia Craig-McFeely

SLG Press
Convent of the Incarnation
Fairacres • Oxford
www.slgpress.co.uk

Printed by
Grosvenor Group Ltd, Loughton, Essex

Contents

Joseph Evans	iii
Introduction	v

Prologue

Winter 15/16	1

I—Icon

Echoes	4
Tree	4
Leaves	5
Dung	7

II—Journeying

Bridges	8
Froth	10
Flag	10
Rome	11
Glasgow Retreat	15
Priest (I)	18
Dutch Kiss	19
The Lusiads	20
Manchester Flamenco	21

III—Word

Adam	23
Jacob	25
Sisera	26
Samuel Today	27
Elijah's Bull	29
Star	30
Cana	31
Jesus Falls the First Time	33
Opus Dei	34
Fish	35

Words	36
Word	38
Dive	39

IV—Hide-and-Seek

Hope	40
Nothing to Say	43
Playtime	43
Bright Grey	44
Corpus Christi	45
Veneremur cernui	46
Flower	47
Inside your Cross	49
Priest (II)	51
Your Silence	53
Subtle	55
The Field	57
The Cross that I Bear Badly	58
Spirit, You are the Fire	59
The Wall	60

V—Chiaroscuro

Silence	61
Everything under Control	61
Velcro	62
Candle	64
Eden, Elsinore, Jerusalem	64
Chocolate Clock	65
The Caged Bird	65
Lost	66
Thief	68
Now	69

Epilogue

Straw	71
Index of first lines	72

Joseph Evans

Father Joseph Evans is a Catholic priest and a member of Opus Dei. Born in Wimbledon, London, in 1966, he grew up in Putney and went to Salesian College Battersea before going to King's College London to study French and Portuguese. He worked briefly as a newspaper journalist in local papers in North East London and Manchester and then as a full-time youth worker for Opus Dei. From 1992 to 1997 he was Director of Greygarth Hall, a university residence in Manchester, and, in this role, in 1994, he co-founded 'Reach Out!', a mentoring charity which seeks to raise the educational and personal aspirations of disadvantaged youngsters. In 1997 he went to Rome to study for the priesthood within Opus Dei and from there moved to Pamplona, Spain, where he did a Masters and Doctorate in Biblical Theology. His doctorate is on a specific theme related to the formation of the New Testament Canon. He was ordained a priest in Rome in 2001 and returned to the UK at the conclusion of his studies.

From 2002 to 2012 he was residential chaplain to Netherhall House in Hampstead, London. In 2004 he joined the Archdiocese of Westminster's chaplaincy team to the universities in London, with its base at Newman House, and was Catholic chaplain to the School of Oriental and African Studies (2004–2008) and the Institute of Education and then Catholic chaplain at King's College London (2007–2017). Between 2012 and 2017 he worked in the Opus Dei Regional Council for Great Britain, with a particular role to support the women members, after which he returned to Manchester to be chaplain of Greygarth Hall. While there, apart from his work with young and married people, he also developed a ministry to fellow priests and the Portuguese-speaking community in that city.

In 2023 he moved to Grandpont House, a students' residence in Oxford under the spiritual care of Opus Dei, which is where he currently resides. He also works extensively with married people and priests, in Oxford and beyond. Once a keen rugby player and cricketer, he now enjoys running, walking in the country, reading, and writing poetry and plays. He loves to teach about the Bible and run Bible study courses. He maintains his journalistic interests and is Co-Founder and Editorial Director of the online magazine *Adamah Media*. He also contributes to, and is priest coordinator for, the podcast '10 Minutes with Jesus'; the podcast 'Into the Deep' offers a selection of his own preached meditations.[1] *When God Hides* is his first published collection of poetry.

---

[1] Available on Spotify, Apple, YouTube, Google Play etc.

Introduction

It is with great joy that I present to the reader this my first ever published collection of poetry. I have written poetry from an early age – it helped to have a mother who was a talented writer, albeit of prose – and she instilled (or rather, inspired) in me a great love of the written word. I still remember, and savour, the joy it gave her when, as a boy, I used the phrase 'pros and cons' in a school essay. Experiences like this are priceless. Or once, when my brothers were teasing me about my literary aspirations, she gently quipped to them: 'Tread softly because you tread on my dreams'. I didn't yet know that line but I sensed it was from a poem and, asking my mother, I discovered it came from the great Irish poet W. B. Yeats.[2] What with affectionate nagging from her and rougher nudges from one of my brothers about my lack of reading (a passion for comics and my father's enthusiasm for sport were most inspiring me at that juncture in my youth), it is no surprise that a love for writing, and with time reading, would come to play an important part in my life. It found expression in poetry, journalism and later in forms of spiritual writing.

These poems were written, with one partial exception, between 2015 and 2023, after almost two decades of very little poetic activity. The Prologue poem 'Winter 15/16' is a reflection on this experience. Why I experienced that dry spell, I cannot say. No doubt my studies in Rome and then Spain and my early years as a priest absorbed me. But my time in the Eternal City did produce a few poems, one of which I consider more significant. This is the above mentioned 'partial exception', namely the poem 'Rome', which I initially wrote when I was studying in that city between 1997 and 1999, that is, as a brief moment of inspiration in this dry period, but I significantly revised it in late 2022 and the start of 2023.

I was living in London until 2017 and it was there that I began to write poetry again. I am a proud and devoted Londoner but most of these poems were written after I moved that year to Manchester, even if they were not

---

[2] From his poem 'He wishes for the Cloths of Heaven'.

all necessarily written in Manchester itself—some were written during trips abroad or on courses or retreats in other places in the United Kingdom. I have always found Manchester a great source of inspiration (the poems of my unpublished 1992–1994 collection 'Above the Troubled Clouds' were all written while I was living in Manchester in an earlier phase of my life) and I want to express publicly my debt to this city. 'Manchester Flamenco' is a sort of tribute to it and its wonderful people. But as I have now moved to Oxford, it seems a good moment to draw this collection to a close.

Some of these poems are very personal and express the situation of my own soul and its struggles. But I have decided to publish them because I believe that they might reflect the struggles of many other people, certainly those who are trying to seek God, and so help them in their spiritual journey. And if my poems do help you, then, please, say a prayer for me.

'Truly, you are a God who hides himself.'
(Isaiah 45:15 ESV)

WHEN GOD HIDES

Prologue

Winter 15/16

I am here, in winter 15/16,
Looking afresh out the window of life;
It seems at last spring is surging anew.
Is the long, barren freeze finally through?
Now rhymes like forest bluebells shoot up, rife
As crime, or as guilty thoughts felt unseen.

For twenty years it seemed I repented,
Kicked the habit, broke the sad addiction.
Was it just want of opportunity,
Or more a lack of ingenuity?
Creaky discourse seemed to conquer fiction;
The Muses' chariot wheels seemed dented.

Just the occasional birthday ditty,
Or the odd poem like the long craved fag
Of the smoker who cannot quite give up;
The alcoholic who needs one last cup,
The bottle badly hidden in his bag,
Seeking an excuse in being witty.

At last the snow has melted, revealing
Instead shoots of new growth, plants pushing
Through hard soil, striving to rise under
The bright sun and even the wild thunder.
No matter! It is light and air, rushing,
Free wind. It is seeing, hearing, feeling!

How long all this will last I cannot say.
I was Zachary made dumb: my own fault,
I am sure, I will not contend or doubt.
Now like Peter's lame man I leap and shout
Inside the temple of creative thought,
With divine John to guide me on my way.

Be this for years or months or merely weeks,
Be this a passing through warbling song-bird,
Be this only a fleeting season that
Allows me to sing my Magnificat,
Makes my voice by heaven's angels heard,
And gives wings to the flight which my soul seeks,

Then praise God, I say, praise God! Yes, let's praise
Him, the giver of gifts, of song and psalms,
The Lord, the giver of life! Praise for time
And the stern bell with its determined chime,
Praise too for beauty and its fading charms,
Praise for life's months, years, minutes, hours and days.

Praise God for the Word which redeems our speech,
And for silence which gives language the space
To be significant, heard and pondered.
Praise for the mysteries which can be wondered,
Sighted, for their thrilling pursuit and chase,
And understanding's thrust and sudden screech;

For what it first grasps and then fails to hold,
The walls it hits and the walls it knocks down;
For being a small spark of divine thought;
For when you laugh at us and count as nought
Our presumed genius, the foolish clown's
'Great idea', or our new joke which is long told.

So praise God for winter, summer, and spring;
For autumnal decline, the leaves falling;
For being his troubadour and cripple,
His mighty wave or scarcely a ripple;
For when speaking or not I am calling
To Him; for song, and when I cease to sing.

I. Icon

Echoes

Perfume of the night; fragrance of the rose
At the sun's full zenith feasting the nose;
The wonder of a cell and all it shows;
A river's roll, as it meanders, slows
Round a bend, gathers pace, then off it goes;
Nature's groaning within time's racking throes;
Light rays refracted through a squirted hose;
Dew's damp freshness drenching old left-out clothes;
A grandmother's wisdom and all she knows;
Poetry's hints, prose's crisp clarity:
The calls, the echoes, of eternity...

Tree

Every tree is a poem
both free verse
and strictly structured
its rhythm the sap
flowing through its wood
the bird-song over seasons
making up new stanzas
And standing underneath it
embraced by its shade
its lonely awaiting my coming
I catch and vocalize its rhyme
as air breathing into it
ever new oxygen

Leaves

Not only their colour and shade, leaves
Are also their dance, choreographed
By the wind, breathed out, expleted, laughed,
As it rejoices, rants, moans or grieves.

The sun too plays her part, joins the dance,
Dressing the leaves in subtle shimmer,
Caressing with a gentle glimmer,
With dazzling sparks which flame and entrance.

The snow too clothes them, in pure attire.
Rain pours down and seeks to flatter
With its insistent pitter-patter,
On their palms tracing its lewd desire.

See how they nod, twitch or idly sway,
Assenting perhaps to your thoughts, or
Just your presence on the stage once more,
Or simply to wish you a good day.

Breeze-bid they now hesitantly bow
Like a sensitive sharing of shame,
Or though they've properly caught your name,
Or as if merely to say '*I know*'.

Like a hand extended to sooth pain,
When the pain is too intense to touch
And the grief felt is too raw, too much,
So the leaves pushed out pull back, refrain.

Sometimes the leaves can seem almost still,
As though they've found power to resist –
Fingers which refuse to be a fist,
Which have finally formed their own will.

But now the branch thrusts out its wild arm,
As a swordsman with fire in his eye
Bares his blade, or a girl dancer's thigh
From its silk folds reveals its full charm.

Then the leaves decide it's time to play,
And with joyful abandon they surf
On windy waves with uncontrolled mirth,
As if this were their task for the day.

And all the while the birds in discreet
Chorus support, like an extra troupe
Of actors, or like a backing group
Enhancing the song with well-timed tweets.

Little the leaves know that they are slaves,
How much they are attached, and how tight
Their leash. Freedom would become their blight,
Their fatal fall to a rotting grave.

Their frolicking and flailing need roots,
Sap, trunk and branch, they are firmly bound,
Reaching skyward yet tied to the ground,
Timed and instrumental to the fruit.

And I? Am I like these leaves, except
I'm flesh and blood, but alike in debt
To my roots and sap, a gem but set?

Am I just a leaf without true wings,
Crafted to dangle on puppet strings,
An inert, if golden, finger ring?

No! I live and think, am fully free,
Was made to leap with the One and Three,
Yet who leaves the dance steps up to me.

Dung

Geese-plopped, pond-side poo.
The perpetrators waddle past
Indifferent to their infraction.

Quick! I am a scientist. Analyze it!
Be the first to discover it.

Quick! I am a busy-body. Report it.
There must be a culprit.

Quick! I am a detective. Examine it.
It could solve the whodunnit.

Quick! I am a mother. Avoid it.
My child might rub his hand in it.

Quick! I am an artist. Paint it.
Surreal, abstract or pre-Raphaelite.

Quick! I am a dog. Eat it.
No bitch will beat me to it!

Quick! I am a journalist. Publish it.
Lest the council try to hush it.

And I? I do nothing quickly.
Like a child learning to read
I slowly decipher the dung's script.

Is it really you
In this pond-side poo,
Expelled, cast out,
But keeping still each station;
Drawing, calling,
Like an icon's invitation?

II. Journeying

Bridges

To John, who at least encouraged me

We must connect, overcome the distance,
Gaps like bleeding scars screaming from the ground,
Bridges to heal these holes, this resistance,
Like so many bandages on a wound.

Why so many obstacles in the way
For boat and car and train and load to cross?
What do all these barriers have to say,
Just what went wrong, what broke, what have we lost?

Our forebears built them in iron and brick,
Practical, sturdy, for progress and gain;
I stand on a footbridge, steel, curved and slick,
Which even shines in the Manchester rain.

This basin once busy with bales and coal
Is now trendy – so chic! – and full of bars;
Leisure not work now nourishes the soul:
The effort was theirs, the fruition ours.

They thought that God would meekly bless their greed.
Now we bless ourselves, living like the rich,
No longer want to recognize our need,
No longer dig, pour water in the ditch.

For now we stand alone, and don't see why
We should take the trouble to pass over.
We can cross the world on our screens, or fly
To distant lands: why, then, should we bother

To slog beside the local man, brother
Of ours in his misery and his sweat?
Not for wealth, work is to stand together,
To pay each other our mutual debt.

But travel still we ought and aim to pass
From one side to the other, though bridges rust
Or fall, for nothing here below can last.
We came from and are made to kick up dust.

John the former punk rocker sits to view
The scene, while an American tourist
Takes photographs. 'What does this mean to you?'
I ask. Both say little, I don't insist

(I wanted them to cross the bridge with me
– A handshake is a bridge or just 'good day' –
I wanted them to see what I could see
– You can't make people think in your own way).

That blood-pouring heaven-dropped ladder-stream
Is a bridge, always building, never done,
Calling us now to climb into its dream:
The ultimate connection, Three in One.

Froth

Chattering and clattering cups,
as Hampstead's young and hip
or idle rich
solve the world's problems
or let it go to rot
over a slow and frothy cappuccino
(the less *engagé*
get a take-away).
Some dive into society's angst
– doppio, lungo, macchiato! –
others hide behind their sip's steam.

Flag

Between the wild air and the turf, the dragon roars,
Red in fury and impotency, the emblem
Of a people's pride, the flowing blood of their wars,
Resisting still today all who have oppressed them.

The flag flutters in the spring's chill and hopeful breeze;
Children wave it, not knowing how little they share
In their land's history and pain, its fields and trees,
How little they have breathed yet of its pure, fresh air.

Now losing hope, its infants are decreasing too;
It clings to trinkets and shiny consumer toys.
Where is the warrior's sword, the preacher's stern fire?
Dear country of my fathers, what has died in you?
O Wales, is a rugby crowd's cheer the only noise
Which can ignite in you a flicker of desire?

Rome

I. *Vallis lacrimarum*

With the first sun, when the tourists come out
like mosquitos, weeds on a triumphal arch,
headless necks of imperial eagles,
all testify to decline.

Rome, waking from winter, remembers
you can't be a jilted empire
and not be a little vain. Traders
at Flaminio sell baseball caps;
Friday is mosque day for Muslims.

Brightness and cloud: so many
shades of failure, from fiasco flash
to dreary drab.
Light and darkness, praise the Lord!
Christ flops here like Jerusalem.

Beauty must stall its extinction,
must fight to survive. *Ragazze,
imparate dalle vostre chiese invecchiate:*[1]
through the years' cracks burns a flame
still seen in aged eyes.

Then does sadness preserve them,
embalmed in grief, the serene sorrow
I feel now? Hope wrapped in sadness,
triumph too, as in Rome's dusty temples.

---

[1] Girls, learn from your ageing churches.

II. *Civitas terrena*

'If you being evil know how...'
Inclined to evil, birthed in pain,
brother-blooding, Lamech-lusting;
evil the civilizing seed, from Enoch,
Jubal and Tubal-cain.

At Augusto's Mausoleum dogs foul,
lovers sneak a snog, drugs are dealt
and consumed, all part of the Emperor's
divine and immortal cult.

Arrogantly alluring,
tell her Bartholomew's tale,
such the way of skin. Daughter of Myriam,
your knoll-like breasts, sun-glazed tan,
one day shall leprous be.

Rejoice, rejoice in liberties acquired!
Free to mine the depths of despair,
to drill new seams of misery,
called progress, gain or enlightenment.

Weep with me the freedoms we have won:
a marriage bond strong as paper glue,
children like ping-pong balls bounced
between two fools or egoists or both.

Mitti the cat has been sought for days.
Oh come back, Mitti, don't be lost;
you make us forget we are evil,
not asking from us too much good.

III. *Civitas Dei*

To know that Peter walked here,
that holy feet of Christian
men and women sanctified in blood
or ordinary life trod these streets.

Let the voices of the saints
rise up through the pavements,
like the Tiber flooding
to wash away all dirt.
Drown me in this history of hope.

Saints and sinners, let us talk:
Interpret this city in your tongue
made mine. In English verbs decode
koine, Latin or speechless sobs.

I must seek a darkness to walk in,
I must lose my grip and my mind,
seek a new language to talk in
to leave mere concepts behind.

IV. *Verbum*

Speak the word which ignites
our hearts, flood-soaked, petrified.
Wilderness-woo us, wash in blood
from blood, the espousing word
which enfleshes love,

The word which whacked Paul,
which won the hearts – chaste, tender
and strong – of Agnes, Cecilia
and Felicity, the word
by which they won;

The word which Monica wept,
mourning in her Roman rest
many modern Augustines,
the word by which Peter returned
upside down to die;

The word which warred in martyrs,
Linus, Clement, Cletus…
the word witty and mirthful
in Neri, Escriva
and *il Papa buono*.

Oh that you would kiss me
with the kisses of your mouth!
Bernini's Teresa seeks those lips.
Divine Breath, my mouth is open,
flame into my parched throat!

Spirit, breathe new winds
into your bride's cancerous lungs,
her tattered sails, new words as ways
to wonder and witness,

the language of silent contrition,
a learning which is watching,
genuflection, heart-stirring,
a language of new beginnings,

gentle irony in the face
of invading empires,
barbarian destruction, internal
corruption and collapse;

words both beautiful and poor:
the language handed down always
(and sometimes only)
by grandmothers mumbling
rosaries in dark corners.

Glasgow Retreat

In quo mihi spem dedisti

Here in this city, what future for God?
Where once cold and damp were ascetical,
Where faith was clear, applied with iron rod,
And enemies were plain heretical.
Even football has lost its tribalism,
Nightclubs are swallowing up the dour kirks,
Thought is too fuzzy for any clear schism:
Forget the creeds, just focus on the perks!
Coffee bars and take-aways rise and fall,
As provincial consumeristic greed
Softens up a once tough people, and all
Indulge, and prefer screens to walk or read.
Now the chill greyness simply depresses,
Talk of independence a distraction
From real issues, which no-one addresses,
And Scotland slips into dull inaction.

Now wet in Bellahouston Park I pray
(Let's not forget: two Popes have here said Mass,
But they have come and gone, and now both days
Are just a date which passed without distress):
Is hope here possible in this ageing
And over-fed race, with unfathered youths?
Can hope survive when apathy raging
Shouts down or smothers the most basic truths?
Is hope, O Lord, still possible in me?
Can my prayer in grimy Glasgow still rise?
Can it still mark the course of history
And penetrate the grim and drizzling skies?
Can I still cup and sip that sating spring,
Which strongly gushing from the Godhead's throne,

Yet struggles through my soul's rock-like, cracking
Hardness, with a creaking, resistant moan?
Fight on I must though little have I fought,
Despair indulgence in this present war;
I have incarnated, do not abort
By breaking the promise which I once swore!

Hope flickers where that silent, trembling flame
Glows quietly to show that He is there,
And, pouring out her woes or family's shame,
Hears a groaning granny in her prayer.
Hope keeps shining when kneeling Christians still
Turn humble eyes to heaven for their needs,
Begging for jobs, exams, the lost or ill,
And old folk meet in church to 'tell their beads';
Where priests in black still hear people's sins, still
Confess their own; where brave couples reject
The contraceptive lie, to know the thrill
Of children's happy cries, and don't neglect
Their frail parents; where a 'real man' stays true
And faithful to his spouse, through thick and thin;
And daily struggling to make their love new,
Each wages war against the snares within.
Hope blazes when believers strive not shirk,
When one man's faith inspires his daily toil,
Where Christian women witness in their work,
And to God and country are likewise loyal.
Hope flames out when that big Glaswegian heart
Displays the warmth and kindness it contains,
Hope will come in new Christian Scottish art
And faith-filled, grace-filled melodious strains.
Hope breathes on when good Glaswegian mothers
With both food and faith their children nourish,
When young souls give up their lives for others…
Then, O then, will Glasgow truly flourish!

O my friend, my child, my father, reader,
Sister, you! Sincere searcher for meaning,
Reading these words you make me a leader,
To guide you towards that deeper cleaning,
I who limp with you, with you fall and rise.
In this cold rain we are together washed,
This drizzle purifies our half-blind eyes,
And our vices are for the moment quashed.
Bathed in God's word, o what delight! Written
Grace, a scriptural foretaste of heaven,
Surrender, friend, your soul like mine, smitten
By such love, such rich, delicious leaven!
Spirit-soaked, washed in sacramental blood;
Spirit-driven, hope fiercely thrusts us on;
Spirit-borne, raised above the earthly clod,
To share in the victory which Christ has won!
And so both in Glasgow and everywhere,
This the anchor and the unbroken rope
We throw up to heaven above the air,
Our unfailing and our unfading hope!

I firmly believe in, truly maintain
This conviction, this light in daily grime.
Yet how difficult hope is, how much pain
To hold on to, how hard a daily climb.

Your mercy is hope, Lord, constant falling
Rain, always cleansing, life-giving, calling.
Amen, and hail to Mary, Virgin Queen,
Through whose mother's heart hope is felt and seen.
Be that mother to us, feed us, nourish.
Now, o now, we pray, may Glasgow flourish!

Priest (I)

Before me a Ford Fiesta,
Delahunty's bar to the left,
all this urban energy, and pettiness,
the fragile wealth, the coffee shops
(those new chapels),
the bubble we call growth.
People walking on the street,
a woman smoking, a child with her dog,
the sleek youth of tourists,
the traffic jam as folk turn homewards,
the sex shop, the yuppy flats,
the rundown buildings,
the closed church,
the gentle evening sun,
the gull's squeal,
the grass' intense greenness
bounded by dull concrete,
the bird on the bench (a living psalm!),
the out of town streets and all their homes
and lives and hopes
and suffering
and sin…
I am priest of all this,
all this for you, and them,
all this a prayer
for blessing or forgiveness,
all this my being, being
chosen, called, created,
for this, and that, and them,

an identity; all this
to be received, processed,
and turned to your glory;
all this an altar, a canticle of praise,
a sacrifice and song.

Dutch Kiss

Your triple kiss, a first
step into
Trinitarian bliss.

Oh that you would kiss me
with the kisses of your
mouth, in Holland, Zeeland,

Friesland, Utrecht, Drenthe…
Many waters cannot
quench love, open your dykes.

Spit out the trinkets in
your mouth, the idols which
fill it and stab your heart,

to make space
for an infinite kiss,
the sweet, fresh breath of love,

lung-filling, delighting
your healed soul
forever.

The Lusiads

In debt to Luís de Camões and Fernando Pessoa

Like small children watching other boys' games,
They lay at Europe's edge, staring, unsure
Where to look: inward at the power play
Or out at the vast ocean main, the way
To greed and glory, through God, pluck and war:
Portugal chose greatness, knew might and fame.

From that Lusitane Western beach they sailed,
Fishermen then fighters, with the sea's brine
As sweat upon their daring, olive chests,
Wives left behind, with children at their breasts,
To sing and suffer, left to fret and pine
For husbands missed and longed for, then bewailed.

So suffering became this people's tale,
And prayer, and joy, and beauty, and feeling
Within the swell's surge, ebb and flow, its mad
Driving back and forth, wished for grief, *saudade*,
Wave-thrown, -thrust, -propelled, current-smacked, reeling
From the surf, knowing big souls do not fail.

They conquered seas by skill and accident,
But didn't learn how power should be held;
They birthed a child which knew too much its will,
Bigger, stronger, but just as frail, Brazil;
And though their ships policed the whole wide world,
All came undone from West to Orient.

Such are these people, shrunken now but still
Warm, loving, proud and passionate, football-
Flamed and hooked, nostalgic, sentimental;
Land-blocked and so sea-staring, nautical;
Mighty once but now puny Portugal,
With yet a call and mission to fulfil!

With their marine, salt-smudged and sea-sent soul,
Simple, raw, not learning, always a child,
Missing what's before them but looking far
(Not for naught were they given Fatima),
Latin both and Celtic, both weak and wild,
With hidden faith driving like the tide's roll.

Manchester Flamenco

Like an ugly wife but with other charms,
You love her deeply though not for the view.
You rest content in her embracing arms,
Plunged in her bosom as in Northern stew.

Head bowed down with stoic grit, she goes dressed
In grey, cheery still in her misery;
She shoulder shrugs, laughs it off with a jest:
'Yes, it's grim up here but I like it, me!'

A red brick surfeit, like rouge on her cheeks,
The rain only causing them more to smudge;
The effect is plain and her clothing reeks,
But she stands firm, and refuses to budge.

Away, I stand and watch, in hot Seville,
A dancer raising tendril-stem wrists,
Flaunting her passion and long-rehearsed skill
In a public square for sun-baked tourists!

Her colleagues sing and clap, serve flamenco
For cash. ¡Olé! Like water down a drain,
She gyrates and twirls. Then the watchers go.
¡Adios! Is shaming part of this art's pain?

No more claps, her folds and fabric unfurled,
Then put away. Perhaps one day she dreamed
Of fame. Manchester is another world.
Her glory too has passed; though great it seemed,

It was cotton-frail, worn and textile thin.
And all for what, this intense industry?
What has the city lost? What did she win?
For what did the workers serve their Queen Bee?

Manchester rains, drizzling her many tears,
For the God she neither found nor renounced.
Her overcast skies are her brooding fears,
The faith she could not refuse or pronounce.

But she also smiles in her city folk,
Warm, kind and open, willing to receive,
Fun and friendly, and ready for a joke,
Generous, big-hearted, able to grieve.

Her hands too weave and form their subtle dance,
Though in cooler climes beneath darker skies;
And though her figure doesn't quite entrance,
The heavens also hear her anguished cries.

Manchester too has her song to sing, sad
And sighing, but not lacking witty quips;
Telling life's tale, with its good and its bad,
Gracefully swaying her sturdy, plump hips.

III. Word

Adam

I am clay, dust,
colour of rust,
earthy, muddy,
soil born, ruddy,
God-like, cursed by sin,
Both male and feminine.

Human from humus,
earthling from the earth,
Adam from adamah.
My (or her) chutzpah
over-played our worth,
caused history's first ruckus.

So fruitful was the soil,
with every type of tree,
so pleasant to the taste,
and oh, so good to see.
But sin made all a waste
and turned my work to toil.

I, Adam, finest fruit
of earth, its choicest crop.
For her I lost a rib,
asleep became a crib,
the deftest divine chop
made me the woman's root.

I, Adam, living mud,
once risen from the ground,
now eaten by its jaws,
it opens for my blood,
and held within its claws
I wake and walk earthbound.

The soil is water,
washing, baptizing
the wheat grain dying;
the rotting, crying,
are fertilizing,
making son, daughter.

Then born anew,
the mud made true,
mankind untrapped
and heaven rapt,
the victory won,
the curse undone.

Jacob

The fighting boy…
He'll wrestle with God Himself,
that man will, and beat Him too,
or trick the good Lord into thinking
that He had lost, though he himself
came out lame and limping.
He snatched his brother's birth-right
for a plate of lentils, deceiving too
his own dying father, blind and fading.
So this is Israel, father of the tribes,
stock of God's own people, proving
that every chosen race is a con,
the Almighty's own choice to be duped,
the game He opts to play
with the wool over His all-seeing eyes,
a hide-and-seek in which He pretends
not to spot the child, poorly concealed
and fully present to His vision.

Sisera

A tent-peg through your temple
is how history records you;
a mighty warrior
stapled to time's floor
by 'frail feminine' arms;
through these, forever stuffed,
divine taxidermy
leaves you dangling
from the Good Book's page:
you were made to be pinned.
Jael, the sweet and buxom host,
the tribal ally, traitor to you,
Israel's hero, God's faithful agent.
So His plans go forward:
power annulled by weakness;
sleep's ambiguous cloud;
the field's wheat and tares;
saints and sinners,
not knowing who are which;
the tent of glory,
the tent of shame;
marvel or murder;
their salvation,
his bludgeoned brain;
milk, rest, and death.
And who am I,
and which should I fear:
Sisera, Jael or the peg?
And might we stand together,
glorious all, by the healing river,
in the heavenly Jerusalem?

Samuel Today

Listen, Lord, your client is complaining,
Just hear me out and note down all I say;
Respond to every grievance, explaining
The reason and redress for each delay.

Speak, Lord, your audience is yawning:
Speak if you must though I've heard it all before;
No fiery words nor urgent warning
Will make me rise to open up the door.

Console me, Lord, your patient is crying,
And is wallowing in pity for himself;
The list of woes is daily multiplying,
From suffered slights to problems with my health.

Answer, Lord, your consumer is detailing
Each and every service you should pay;
State, please, your plan to deliver, if by mailing
Or fulfilling my desires some other way.

Act, Lord, your patron is expecting
His list of intentions to be swiftly met;
With prayer so clear, so lucidly directing,
Surely what I ask for I should get.

Reply, Lord, your public is demanding,
Your power if it's real must meet my needs;
I won't believe if you're not commanding,
If faith can't produce effective deeds.

Speak, servant, your lords are awaiting
Verifiable results with data proof,
Answers which we can then start debating,
To decide ourselves if we'll call them truth.

Speak, I say! You'd best have a reason
For making children work in temple tasks,
Leaving their home before due age and season;
Why should priests heed what a mother asks?

Speak to explain why Eli had to perish:
Why ask a father to reprimand his sons?
They were just young men who wanted to relish
Pretty young flesh and a bit of fun.

Listen, Lord, your servant is aching,
So much deceit is too heavy a load;
I've done with religion which is merely faking,
A futile drive down hypocrisy's road.

Listen, Lord, and accept this mess,
This muddled dog's dinner of my bitty prayer;
Accept the guilt which I now confess,
My madman's ravings to the boundless air.

Listen, Lord, your son is crying
Streams of remorse at last sincere;
Truth's first steps, the end of lying,
The start of love and loss of fear.

Listen, Lord, your child is chattering,
Talking away with a toddler's glee;
Can you hear and see the door I'm battering,
Begging you to stay close to me?

Hush, dearest Father, for your child is sleeping,
So bear me gently in your warm embrace;
Carry me heavenward, I've ceased my weeping,
You can wipe the tears from my smiling face.

Speak, Lord, your servant is listening,
Calm in your hands like a trusting bird;
His ears alert and his eyes glistening,
To hear and fly on your saving word.

Elijah's Bull

I lie here, Spirit, awaiting your fire,
I am Elijah's soaked and cut up bull,
So damp and passionless seems my desire;
It is the trench around the altar, full
Of water, impossible to ignite.
I am the priests of Baal, dancing in lust
For any pretty thing catching my sight,
Foolishly prancing in circles of dust.
How long, then, limp in this frustrating state?
How long rave, wounding myself in this way?
How long crave for idols I can control?
Be no sleeping god, no lie, do not wait;
Answer me now, oh Lord, do not delay.
Blaze Trinitarian flames in my soul!

Star

How cruel, star, to be subject to our will.
What vicious and sadistic game you play!
That we must want to see you, we must choose
To let your glory in beyond the sill
Of our mind's free sight, that you will obey
Us humbly, will bow to and not abuse
Our self-determined vision, accepting
To be seen or not, just as we decide.
And how perverse again to disappear,
And again once more, always expecting
Us to follow on and on, through the wide
Expanses of darkness, seeking both near
And far for unclear answers, so taking
Unsure steps, always uncertain, thinking
But never knowing, never fully found.
Always nocturnal, dodging the waking
Hours; at times, it seems, tauntingly winking,
But never fully marking out the ground;
Or part-illumining the path, sparing
In the light you give, only a star's glow,
Never the sun's dazzle, making us need
Companions on the road, others caring
To share and light our way, torches, fellow
Travellers, needy too, forcing us to heed
The wise advice of those who have read more,
Who know but may not join you, may not dare,
And to seek rest and food in risky halls;
Carelessly, it seems, leading to that door
Where the Star Himself sleeps peacefully, where
Light Himself lies among animal stalls.

Cana

There is a yes which is no and a no which is yes,
for language only scratches at the heart's yearning.
A resistance to act becomes action and glory,
the rejection of an hour the fullness of time,
for time is no longer mere loss and condemnation,
the withering of fruit on the trees,
the day's dreary decline,
it is now both bud and blossoming, anticipation,
a glimpse and gulp of glory through opened skies,
from monotonous to messianic,
thus the beginning of festival
to accelerate heaven's arrival.

And so sterile time is fructified and fermented
through an exchange of glances, divine eyes
yielding to human, because the woman
though woman is yet woman (or rather, Woman)
and God too desires her beauty.
But above all she is mother and so
like God all-powerful, both as mother
and for having conceived the Word
as her body's soul fruit.
What words cannot express
desire achieves, a pause becomes power,
her delay to respond, assimilating
the refusal, accepted in prayer
but in prayer rebutted and overcome,
makes silence omnipotent.

Willingly I am caught in that cross-fire of love,
the space between eyes, breath and hearts,
between son and mother, God and creature,
the space of seconds, the infinite space
of human hesitation, the space of her doubt
resolved into determined action,
for my constant negations
to become, at her insistence,
God's action in me
and for this unclean water
to be spirited into alcohol and flavour.

As Word became flesh, so it made water wine.
What was flowing through history,
trickling in tight, rocky beds
and dark, underground channels,
in constant threat of drought,
has now found the distant ocean
which it always sought
and which at last came to it.
What was imprisoned in stone jars,
inert, passive, for uncertain purification,
now pours from them into human throats,
giving joy at last to men's hearts,
graced but awaiting its later fulfilment,
in a poor clay chalice
through a soldier's spear
the gushing out of blood.

Now it just needs the stewards,
sensitive to her sweet command,
servant of servants but imperative,
to fill and draw unconscious
of the greatness of their role,
but sanctifying their ignorance

by filling to the brim
to make the wonder greater.
The careless groom is rewarded
by the best wine at the last,
and so history is reborn
as it is repeated, all things made new
when all seemed about to end.

Jesus Falls the First Time

As He fell, so it all falls apart;
our dreams of grandeur
a blood-sweat puddle on the ground,
the scraping of wounds against gravel,
the thud of the fall,
a kick, a whip-lash, a curse,
success sucks the soil.
How many of my endeavours
have bitten dust,
lie crushed under their own weight,
pant in pain,
grovel in shame.
Once again it is all over.
Then His muscles tense
and with laboured breath
He begins to rise.

My own fall is slower:
I go down in stages,
a phased collapse,
the bland weakening of my knees,
or I slip over a supple form.
My fall might become a siesta,

I lie prostrate with a pillow,
I even enjoy the dirt
and use as a cushion the cross
(which I padded before starting).
My first time is my five thousandth,
If I ever really left the floor;
at best I might crawl ahead.
Jesus falls again
for my slowness to rise.

Opus Dei

He hangs, *Opus Dei*;
A breeze tickles His armpit:
It is accomplished.

His death is *opus Dei*,
To the end, to the extreme,
Love to the last breath.

He is the *Opus Dei*,
Where the divine and human
Meet and forge grace.

All work, *opus Dei*,
Is feminine too,
So she stands too by the Cross.

The wide open sky
Is the Spirit's brushwork,
Framing murder into art.

All work is art, *opus Dei*,
The number cruncher's
And the hole puncher's.

All is silent,
Over the whole land.
Only love's panting can be heard.

His Spirit-gasps sing love,
Make art, through her pierced heart,
All making *opus Dei*.

Fish

Water like a tomb, stone-closed.
No fish-life stirs beneath the cold grey slab
Of its impenetrable darkness, drab
Like death. But just as He rose

One early morning, as day
Was breaking, out of night, at crack of dawn,
A first breath of life, the first struggling yawn
To fight its determined way

Out of mankind's sinful, bored
Sleep, tingles on the chilled and rigid lake,
Which suddenly, once fishless, now awake,
Throbs beneath the boat now moored,

Till then immobile, though near
To eternity's shore where rest His feet,
His divine toes hugging the sand's soft heat,
And His voice, which all can hear,

Speaks both question and a wish,
Which only love can see and understand,
Though faith is first to dive and swim for land:
'Children, have you any fish?'

Words

One word
after another.
Another one butts in
– listen to me! –
demanding urgent
and selfish attention.
And so each word is a child,
and each one insecure,
always seeking company,
as always profoundly lonely.

But words too are bricks,
and take the weight,
bear the burden,
hold back for others to shine.
Words bond and build.

Words are water,
refreshing and renewing
when not drought or flood.

Word is call,
it makes community
(silence its necessary frame,
as painted figures need a background);
it fears senselessness and seeks meaning,
its integrity abused by the madman's raving;
word seeks its complement in sign
and sign its fulfilment in reality.

Word is worship,
rising beyond itself
through the faith of ages
with divine nuances

and its efficacy of action
making word event,
human, limited
and infinite.

The loss of words is the loss of life,
the keyboard's mass production
adds little to truth
in this digital diarrhoea.
Yet so powerful are words
that surprising crops still surface
on this sea of man's manure.

Words electrified
mean lives accelerated,
the tyranny of electronic type
leaves us no time to talk;
close contact confuses
and so may lead to sex,
erotic contradiction
between bodily
and personal intimacy.
No wonder salvation
can only be
a Word made flesh.
The same breath and lips
which make words
also make kisses,
and a kiss can be for love or lust.

Words can be gift or grab,
verity or verbiage,
to serve or to flatter;
may mine – to God, to you –
be always the former
and never the latter.

Word

Words slide across meaning,
skating its smooth surface,
dusting over depths,
labelling life;
here being has been,
slipped from grasp,
the word left behind,
blew away – puh!
This noun merely an echo
of being's erstwhile presence,
an external observer,
an astronomer catching faintly
the star's ancient glimmer;
this verb the hollow shell
of action too subtle to spell,
intensity beyond conjugation.

Words skid across meaning,
embarrassed in their abundance,
more revealing less,
crash into confusion,
hurtling in horror
down a speech-dug chasm.

Words scrape across meaning.
Only one speaks it,
is it.

Dive

Not everything we see can be written down;
we must free ourselves from the tyranny of speech.
Speaking requires clear and specific terms;
not saying is fruitful:
it is to accept, to wait for being to reveal itself to us
in its own time, on its own terms,
giving it the opportunity
to fill our soul's hole.
To let be is almost to create.
There are impressions that fly above
or dive below words
or drown in the choppy waters of confusion.
I see you and do not hear,
I hear you and do not see,
hearing and seeing do not go together,
one goes behind the other,
running to catch up.
I digest the word
through my eyes.
Your word
more than word
is a kiss.
And with that, without speaking,
it says it all.

IV. Hide-and-Seek

Hope

I can only hope. It is the ferry
Across the foggy water, at its prow
A weak torch, pushing through damp, chilling air,
Slow but determined and dourly merry.
Hope is both vision and grappling with now,
Both taking this step and ready to dare.

I can only hope. Preceding both love
And faith, it tiptoes discreetly ahead,
Sure that one day it will firmly believe,
Throws its anchor heavenward, looks above,
Trusts that it too can yet rise from the dead
To live what it daily fails to achieve.

I can only hope, though cracked deep inside,
Crumbling rock, shaky in my foundations,
I walk tottering, stand swaying, at times
Lurching wildly, often brought down by pride,
Crashing groundward, but Christ in three stations
Fell for me, to pick me up from my crimes.

I can only hope, though evil empires
Rise and fall, and arise ever again,
Though the wicked seem always in control
And proud ignorance constantly inspires
Endeavours which deceive, corrupt, and then
Destroy for ever many human souls.

I can only hope. It is my unique
Defence against despair's constant attacks,
from brutal assaults to discouragement,
To bury me in a crushing and bleak
Suicidal landslide, with just a few tracks
On its surface, paths of failed intent.

I can truly hope, because in a tomb
Lies a corpse, cold, bloodied, but not rotting,
Closed in by a stone, soldiers standing by.
That sealed-up cave breathes life, it is a womb,
It exudes power above man's plotting,
It will explode with saving energy!

I can joyfully hope, because she, pure
Virgin and Spouse, stands, grace's victory,
As the unconquered one, restricting sin.
She who never doubted, whose faith assures
Our own. Her life brings hope to history.
In her, through her, we see we all can win.

I can firmly hope because a man-rock,
Though at times himself more a stumbling stone,
Though prone to run away and to deny,
Still stands to resist hell's violent shock,
Still shouts above Satan's despairful moan,
Still proclaims truth with an unending cry.

I can live in hope because the grammar
And foundation of all being, its code,
Are love and mercy, infinite, divine.
Because the Spirit transforms the stammer
Of our poor prayer, while the Son bears our load
And turns our dirty water to sweet wine.

I feed on hope because the Eucharist
Renews my strength each day, and silently
He waits for me and hears. The flickering
Lamp is hope. However much we resist
His gentle calls, and however badly
We treat Him, His grace gives life, quickening.

It sparks desire for virtue, appetite
For His love, refusing to go away.
In Confession He forgives, resurrects,
Turns crushing sin to fading mist, dawn light
And breeze blowing away the guilt, the day
Conquering night, healing all He inspects.

I hope because the tomb is empty, bare,
Just linen and angels, the boundless space
Of Divine Life. Satan screams, the rock-jaw
Gapes open, the priests scratch their heads, fresh air
Blows, the wind, flowing gustiness of grace.
The rolled-up head-cloth cries hope from the floor.

I hope to be a saint, make this desire
My ardent goal, believe it within reach,
Trust in your gifts, your unfailing promise.
This holy ambition which you in-fire
Is possible because you, True One, teach
It, spark it through your Spirit's flame and kiss!

Nothing to Say

I have nothing to say, and you likewise
Play dumb in stubborn silence. So are you
Also sulking? Have you decided to
Punish my lukewarm and half-hearted cries
With a sky both grey and rainless, dropping
Down not dew from above, but emptiness
From within, till I should face and confess
My soft mediocre sin as stopping
Communication, clouding over both
Sun and stars? What earthly desire, what lust,
Petty and fireless, this time again must
Be unmasked to reach the next step, the growth,
Which patiently you daily offer me?
What must I accept to set my prayer free?

Playtime

You are not talking, your silence
Seems like a rebuke, shifting blame
Back to me, a mute but intense
Refusal to pronounce my name.
Faith becomes hugging a spirit,
Clutching at disincarnate air,
Mouth open, nothing to fill it,
Yet trusting still that you are there.

From that veiled casque, while watched you watch,
Your power acts immobile, still.
In darkest night, your subtle touch
Rouses my soul with a sweet thrill.

Must it be so, always the same,
Love whispered in a divine game?

Bright Grey

Here in this bright greyness, in this mild chill,
With spring pulling free from March's tight grip
Like a small child determined to play will
In the hot-blooded passion of youth rip
Himself free from granddad's cold, cautious hand,
I struggle once again to heed your call.
My soul roams mapless through a misty land,
With faint echoes of your heavenly hall.

I cannot see the heights you point me to
And so wander in the mud-flats, reaching
Only the odd hillock with signs of you.
Nor do I hear your voice, for your teaching
Is always soundless, or in blurred pictures,
Or traces of your past passage, like fire's
Remains, some left scraps, a former fixture,
And confused sentiments of deep desires.

But as always you trick me in this game,
I never know who does the hide-and-seek,
Who conceals himself, and who calls whose name,
Who wins the wrestle, who is strong, who's weak.
The progress is never smooth, the going
Always slow, I slip back, fall, sometimes lurch
Ahead, tip-toe forward, but yet knowing,
As lost as I am, love is in the search.

Each day you caress me, show me the way,
Your silence within me still softly sings.
Each day you call me to come out to play.
Each day I fly safely upon your wings.

Corpus Christi

Crisp. Crunchy.
Calling
Quietly. Converting.
Calm. Comfort.
Confessed, Christ creeding.
Consecrated.
Banquet. Sacrifice. Sacrament.
Crucified, killed, quickened, coming.
Communion. Kiss.
Consumed. Consummating.
Psyche catering,
Corporal curing. Sanctifying.
Continuous contentment.
Glorification.
Angelic choirs.
Contemporary.
Accompany.
Tabernacling.
Country, cosmopolis, catholic.
Sacred. Mystic. Creative.
Architecting, canto,
Sculpture, culture.
Caritas. Care.
Queen coated.
King incrumbed,
Captured,
Encountered,
Compliant.
Concealed.
Covert apocalypse.
Encrypted Kyrios.

Joseph Evans: *When God Hides*

Veneremur cernui

The monstrance glass like a diver's mask
    invites to plunge
    to Divine Depths
– or swim like Peter quickly clothed
    to eternity's shore
    (the altar a ledge
    at the cliff's base).
This infinite ocean of tomb-bursting love –
    saving tsunami! –
which as love must be relation and life
    and so Trinity;
this laddered lowering of love,
God who becomes flesh,
flesh which takes the form of bread,
blood-sweat poured out through wine,
teaches true religion which must become
the fullness of gift, sacrifice of self,
forgiveness even in breathless desolation,
love which is stronger than death,
    as true love must be,
throbbing with tenderness and power,
love which truly lives forever
and raises up the loved one…
    Only this is love.
    Into this I dive:
        Tantum ergo!

Flower

For N.Y. and other brave souls

Flower, you poke your fragile head up through the soil,
And seeing so much air, you almost die of fright.
You look back to earth's shelter, the dark, clinging night
Where, suffocating safely, your inner turmoil
Can snugly rot in sweet familiar despair.
There, feeding on itself, like insects you know well,
It finds a comfortable corner in this hell
And gasps tuberculoid sobs in its putrid air.

Child, do you not know you were made to reach the skies?
The slow corruption of our form, its undoing,
Is yeast-like creation, glorious renewing,
Making dull inert mass freshly, tastily, rise.
Choose your darkness, daughter: anguish ever growing,
Burrowing ever more down into the grim gloom,
Or your Father's house with its chosen, furnished room,
Through the blinding, painful – destroying! – unknowing
Of the Spirit's touch, His hand covering our eyes,
His burning, purifying, sanctifying fire,
The cooking – grilling, boiling, roasting – of desire,
Making ever more child-like our soul's deepest cries.

Flower, you must face the fury of the winds and storms,
Which start inside, your flimsy foundations shaking.
It is the Cross, death, agony, an unmaking
Of oneself, uprooting, casting away the worms
You relied on up to now, those blind, senseless friends.
You are being ripened, harvested, plucked, freed, shed,
To enter the banquet as food and to be fed
By the love which, once your daily wheat, never ends.

Little one, great if you accept this, though your groans
Seem muffled beneath many layers of thick, packed mud,
Buried you are already the start of a bud;
In those depths too nature – supernature – intones
Its hymn. To pray even when fighting to believe
You are heard can be the greatest prayer, the deepest
Faith. When prayer gives no peace, no joy, no light or rest,
Prayer that is pain, Christ's sweat of blood, making you grieve
More intensely, but loving with greater power,
Love in His, redeeming, love far greater than sin,
Love that never loses, love which will always win,
Love always bearing fruit, love always in flower!

Do not go back, slithering down scared to your roots:
They were made to push up and out, to force and fight,
They were made to struggle bravely to reach the light!
They were made to be stalk and ear, or branch and fruits.
The Risen One rose to take us from the mud's tomb,
To make us fertile seed, yeast, powerful leaven,
To glimpse now and possess the kingdom of heaven,
To make the heavy brown earth a life-bearing womb.

'Where is God in this darkness, in this black, cold mist?'
But, girl, the whole sky hugs you, its air embracing
You in its fresh breeze. The Spirit's wind is racing
To make you live and breathe anew, thrive, re-exist.
Already now, young one, you are daily made new
And Mary by the Cross births you ever again.
But in the next life, reborn spirited flesh, then
Grace will wrap, transform you in its infinite blue!

Inside your Cross

For K. E.

Inside your Cross, your wounds, inside
Your heart, I am lost, not knowing
My way around, without bearings.
I would like to run away, hide
In some safe place. You are showing
Me the path for those more daring.

I am no mystic, special seer
With wondrous spiritual gifts.
Mine is an everyday entrance
Into your pain, just normal fear
Of the hard, cleansing grace which lifts
Us to sanctity, rough and dense;

This thicket of deep union with
You, the pricking and cutting thorns,
The darker and more cloudy view:
I baulk at what you want to give,
And struggle against being shorn
Of the old man to be the new.

My Cross, not yours, is often pride,
Or resisting the daily tasks,
Or lack of love, all smarting stings;
Your purifying grace applied
Heals and comforts but also asks
Whether I will accept your wings.

These offer me a higher love,
To take me up onto the Cross,
To die more to live each day more.
These wings are both eagle and dove,
They are the slow on-going loss
Of past securities, hope's door.

Through it we reach heaven losing
All we once counted good below.
They are delay, or the unknown,
Uncertain future, not choosing
Our path, having meekly to grow
By tending crops we have not sown;

When God does not seem to reply,
All seems just interrogation,
With no answer, whisper or light;
Or when there seems no reason why,
Not a hint of explanation,
And life one black and endless night.

These wings are feeling unsuited,
The sense of always being wrong,
Not up to it, lacking the skills,
Or feeling exiled, not rooted,
Speaking badly a foreign tongue,
And missing home and native hills.

They are our poor, wounded nature,
Our various lusts, still crying
To live on, refusing to die;
Our weakness as fallen creatures,
Our poor heart's pitiful sighing,
Its latest sentimental lie.

I look at your Cross from outside
Both wanting and not to go in.
But I am in your wounds, now, deep
Within them. Holding on I ride
Upon your Cross bearing our sins,
On you, with you, in you, I weep.

My tears, my pain, are rather yours.
You make your home inside my wounds
And give me penance so gently.
Man of bruises and swelling sores,
Raise me up always from the ground
And then carry the Cross for me.

Priest (II)

He comes into view,
colour black like soil,
for other lives
to grow, and God.

Other lives…
From his dark and luminous denial,
they live and work,
and love and wed,
rear children and change,
and change the world.
Others. All held
In his unclasping hands,
coarse and fruitful as a farmer's.

Sunday is his world,
the Sabbath rest
his weekly test;
then daily deaths and meetings,

children and the sick,
the lost or searching,
open heart surgery in a sterile box,
cutting and purifying,
a sacred amputation,
the spoken kiss of life.

The pouring in of God
to start their days,
and oil to close them,
lubricating them for eternity.
The daily demands, or lack of them:
the women who still come;
the men who keep away,
unless they're hungry.

He pours out as he is filled himself,
gushing or serenely flowing;
when not, he's drained,
dries up, cracked and broken
like a dry, weary land, waterless, polluted.

His words unpolished,
which the Divine Wind takes
and magnifies and moves around,
changing their meaning,
and then, and only then,
the seed settles and takes root.

A mustard bush with scraggly
unplanned branches
for many nests and claws
which grip his heart and flesh,
attached to fragile frames
made, sometimes it can seem,
to defecate upon him.

But their fluttering around you
makes everything worthwhile,
their taking off and flying back,
their nesting and departure,
their return, their cheerful tweeting,
their angry squawking,
their flight to the skies.
The eagles which you, poor sparrow,
have begotten.

And again those claws
which cling to you
and make you almost feel
as if you're strong and needed.
Then the bishop moves you,
or you die.

Your Silence

Your silence
Convicts, a mute accusation,
The process is constant and always the same,
The unspeaking presence –
Eternally right! –
You say nothing and I am to blame.

Your silence is the womb,
The sleeping hush,
The unheard, life-filled breath;
Your silence is unstated understanding,
The knowing look after all these years,
And the silence of ending, closure,
The stony silence of death.

Your silence, like green, has many tones,
It is like a tree's shade
Or the low whoosh of distant traffic.
It acts as a restful backdrop,
To be punctured by a cough.
One enters it hopefully,
Like a glade.

Like a glade it is dark,
Or dimmed, with occasional
Rays of light
Piercing the gloom,
Shining on a leaf-veiled path;
It is the end's glimmer,
The shimmer of dawn,
It most resounds at night.

Silence is the heart's sincerity,
Its honest inner gaze,
Silence will not settle on deceit;
It skims over superficiality,
Its dew won't fall,
It eschews excess
Of damp, cold or heat.

Your silence pierces,
Reveals dust and disease,
Cuts and caresses,
Questions, invites, consoles.
Your silence transforms,
Heals hearts, sows peace,
Turns minds into souls.

Subtle

I cannot be subtle
    I go full-throttle
        I reach for the bottle
    My poetry
Planting and pruning
The branching and gnarled me

I cannot be subtle
      Drop a hint
      A sudden glint
Suggesting hoarded hidden gold

I cannot be subtle
    The finest point
        The thinnest joint
    A wall's crack
With a covert cave behind
A nuanced glance
    Feeling's flash
A world's window
    Beyond phrases
Narrating through gaps

I cannot be subtle
    As I'm a man
    And do what I can
    And growl and bark
    And deal in fists and hammer blows
    And loudly cough and blow my nose

I cannot be subtle
    That faint flush
        Her sizing sight
            A word left feather-floating
    A telling look
Silence speaking
    The sphinx-like smile
    The escaped tear held
Her power in pity and pain
The heart's sign language
        Delicately fingered

I cannot be subtle
The tracery of mist
    Escaping sight
    Evading grasp
Nor paint the first fading
    Glimmer of dusk
Catch Autumn's last fling of light
Its dying dazzling defiance

I cannot be subtle
        Sculpt pain
Chisel loneliness and longing
    It takes a genius
To construct emptiness

I cannot be subtle
The church's hush
      People sitting
        The Spirit stirring
      The flow of incense through air
Its smoky prayer

I cannot be subtle
Sketch the surging seed
The passage of seasons
      Spite's barb
The savour of sauce

I cannot be subtle
 Because I am a child
   And a dog
 Because I hope and trust
And even when I suffer
 I laugh out loud
And trustingly run to your arms

The Field

The field stretches before me, its restful
Greenness inviting me to peace, each blade
Of grass insistent that it has seen all
Before, that though flowers wither and fade,
New shoots arise, new blossom, and its mud
Instructs me to submit serenely, in
Life's frequent downpours, to the latest thud
Of boots which tread its soil, and to begin
New planting, always seeking better fruits.
The field stares dumbly at me, as fields stare;
Eternal seems its grass in shallow roots,
Eternal seems the quickly passing air.
As I look, it looks back blindly at me.
And your eternal love is what I see.

The Cross that I Bear Badly

The Cross that I bear badly but I bear,
The cloak of daily failure that I wear,
The graces and the setbacks that I waste,
The tasks I hold back from, my sinful haste,
The weakness within, the chaos without,
Disorder, delays, the repeated rout
Of resolutions made but not fulfilled,
The unachieved goals, the good I had willed,
The softness of the flesh, the heart of stone,
My soul's disgust and my conscience's groan,
The ambitious pride with its stupid schemes,
The desire for fame, idiotic dreams,
The vain fool fancying himself a saint,
The artless future my vanity paints,
Reluctance to accept the here and now,
The many years with so little to show,
The virtue not attained, the work not done,
Struggles abandoned, battles lost not won,
Heavenly plans against which I rebelled,
Those many times I sulked, bemoaned or yelled,
The tedious, ungrateful complaining,
Always thinking it was cold and raining,
Seeing only the clouds and not the sun,
Feeling a victim and not having fun,
The good desires I did not carry through,
All those projects I did not start to do,
The doubts, not trusting and resisting grace,
My lazy, reluctant and ambling pace,
The countless times that I failed to show love,
When I acted like a hawk not a dove,

The fickle resolve, the wandering eyes,
Self-dissatisfaction, frustrated cries,
Self-satisfaction and enjoying praise,
Not firm or committed in many ways…
Thus far, dear Lord, is my life history,
I can only cry 'Have mercy on me!'
But in all I omitted or did wrong
Your power in my weakness was made strong.

Spirit, You are the Fire

Spirit, you are the fire, the igniter
Of Elijah's soaked and squidgy carcass,
The wind-flame of Pentecostal rumpus,
You are the blood in the sacred writer's
Veins, the pulse of his willing creation,
The sparking of his intelligent mind.
You are the meaning when we look behind,
You are ever-active innovation!
Will you not then work in me? Could you fail
To turn my dampness to a holocaust
Of blazing offering, up thrust, love-forced
By the infinite desires I inhale
Within your breezy and whispering sphere?
Shout if you must into my wax-clogged ear!

The Wall

This wall I cannot climb, or so it seems,
Which hems me in and follows all my ways,
And blocks the flight and hopes of all my dreams,
Looks down on me and out from my own gaze.

This wall I cannot climb transparent stands,
You watch me closely from the other side;
I hear you, see you, feel you, and these hands
Could hold yours tight across the thin divide.

This wall I cannot climb is in my heart,
A barrier in me I cannot cross,
A rock-like rampart formed to keep apart
The inner me and those beyond the fosse.

This wall I cannot climb is made of ice,
A coldness deep within, a frozen cage;
It's not a wicked baseness or a vice,
More frigid chill than any blazing rage.

This wall I cannot climb has rocks too high
Which form the route but lie beyond my reach;
So either place my hands or make me fly,
To show the way which only you can teach.

This wall I cannot climb is not that high –
Your love will be the air which makes me rise.
Then lift me up and over when I die,
Above the wall and up beyond the skies!

V. Chiaroscuro

Silence

Your word is silence, wrapped in pain's darkness,
Joy like the timid sun glimpsed through dark clouds.
Hope is simply desire for a life less
Burdened, less anxious, without the wild, loud
Raving of violence, Satanic screams
Shouting down always faith's gentle appeal.
Why is it so reasonable to dream
Of Love's triumph while seeming so unreal?
Fidelity is always stress, too much
To do, too few to help, always to fail,
Free seats at table, the wounded man's crutch,
Always an incomplete, unfinished tale,
But always, too, lives touched, raised from the earth,
Grateful faces, hearts healed, the soul's re-birth.

Everything under Control

We have everything under control,
    Mankind mastered,
Functioning format achieved,
    All systems operational.

        Truth is data,
        Faith is fact,
    Science has abolished sin,
    Our saints are statisticians.

Empirical research now shows
Results are right, the new might,
But to be ignored at will
    When certitude clashes with caprice,
    When we make ourselves gods,
    When we cannot control our whim.

Velcro

Buttons are too binding
Their slit subjugation
Seems almost colonial.

Zips mimic marriage
And its antique oppression
Two lives too tightly clasped
By locked teeth
Biting into each other.

Buckles are for ancient buccaneers
Suggesting heavy belts
Fettering the waist
Definitely not desired
By modern mores.

Hooks are hateful
They point to pirates
And cruel steel
Cutting into flesh.

The metal hook and eye
Most certainly outdated
Awkward to handle
Resisting swift release.

Laced fastening can fail
Leaving you literally
Tied together
In a tricky knot
It simply won't do
or undo.

Snap fasteners suck you down
Swallowing freedom
Removal should always be trivial.

Magnetic fasteners
Signal power
We can't control
Not to be recommended.

Only Velcro comes undone
With an effortless tug
Temporarily bonding
But with easy extrication
And no wounds to heal.

The liberated surfaces
Meet and depart
With no hard feelings.

Hail Velcro the fastener of our age!

Candle

Tame flame signalling silence in peaceful prayer,
The gleam and warmth of romance, intimacy's glow,
Fire captured and controlled, heat harnessed, light lassoed,
Flickering, fragile, breath-threatened, breeze-quenched,
Wax-wound wick, fickle quivering hope, trembling
Almost naively in the surrounding gloom,
Like a child's innocence, fearing the black night's
Rancid and stifling breath, dancing always
With death in smooth and supple twitches, shooting smoke
Even in its most vibrant motions, in its most
Glaring, dazzling grace knowing its certain fate,
Condemned to end sad and solitary stubble.

Eden, Elsinore, Jerusalem

Would I woo you with words,
toxic spell in your willing ear,
breath floating over fresh skin?
Suddenly you are deaf and wrinkled,
your eternal youth yet another lie,
And only the first bite was tasty.
I drank the poison, then poured
The potion into you.
Fidelity's blank verse,
Vaccine to the curse,
Antidote in advance;
Its plain passion like shoots
Climbing up through dark soil.

Chocolate Clock

My chocolate clock is melting
The white bits have run down
What once was so exciting
Is now a sorry frown

I thought it was so clever
To have a clock so sweet
I really didn't ever
Envisage this defeat

I thought that my life always
Sugary would be
I thought that all the doorways
Would open wide to me

But soured now by guilt
I age and feel life's shock
Wishing I had built
Upon more solid rock.

The Caged Bird

This cagèd bird, crumb pecking,
Flapping intensely its wings,
Striking the bars with their force.
Outside are the heights of love,
The bird's fear is its own cage.

Lost

Lost, like a trapped animal:
the terrain is known,
the context new;
racing around
the imprisoning perimeter,
uncomprehending
how once free space
is now a predatory assault.
Halting at last
from this chased chasing,
I can only hiss
with shoulders and neck contracted
and eyes focussed on an unseen enemy;
I do not know when or what to pounce at.
I am lost in your silence
and my deafness,
yet always wanting to hear.
Is the thorn your goad
or my carnality?
Is the Trinity too much
and the host too small,
too quiet and too still?
Yet I know no answers lie
in rebellion and anger,
and your battered, beaten Church
(with self-inflicted wounds),
ageing in these parts
and ever greyer
(we must rebuild the walls),
commands still belief

for defending, only she
(oh good Mother!),
the life that is her founder's
as living, risen God,
from womb to ancient years.
Resist the contraceptive lie,
the greatest lie,
the slow and comfortable suicide
which leaves us too frail
and sad to pace around the cage,
too impotent even for anger.
What am I sorry for
and what do I seek?
Who am I sorry to?
Can you expect guilt's confession
if you hide away?
How can I apologize
if you disappear?
I too can plead for Sodom
and find you retreating
like an army scorching the earth:
you give way and I am defeated.
How can I be so lost
and be slowly finding myself,
like clues to my own identity,
little white stones which gradually
piece together my eternal name?

Thief

I pray, you block, like a cricketer
Nightwatchman, sent only to maintain
The order. To my constant falling
You just stand by watching, a mute stare.
I am biblical ground without rain.
You respond by stubborn stonewalling.

But I am false and my blame unfair.
Calling so weakly should I complain
Not to be heard? Drinking from dirty
Pools, why do I wonder to find there
The muck which then pours into the drain
Of my soul, the doubt which so hurts me?

Give me the faith I lack, cure the rust
Which, crippling, makes me crumble and creak;
Heal my poor heart which poacher-like hunts
What is not mine to take. Grace me trust
In you at last, eyes to see, to seek
You, fired by Spirit-prayed sighs and grunts.

Love, I steal your beauty, and my heart
Clutches at straws of fake happiness.
Exchanging performance for belief,
I am cheated by counterfeit art.
Mercy me, cross-hung king; I confess
That I too am the repentant thief!

Now

Now that I can't talk to you,
that you don't answer back;
now that I cry childishly
for sweets and fresh fruit,
and am beaten down
by poisonous desires,
succulently rotten and false;
now that prayer is throwing stones
into a hushed, all-swallowing lake;

now that love must only be
patient acceptance
of an established bond,
the forged in-flaming,
the mutual grafting of years:
no longer chase or hunt,
the obsessive passion
of excited Eros,
but the acceptance and avowal
of fragility and failure;

now that love is no longer success,
not even desire, just plain
and dry commitment,
a multi-coloured masterpiece
hidden beneath drab magnolia,
a statue in bits (be it broken
or in construction, I cannot tell);
now that it is a mute symphony,
poetry without words or rhyme,
lacking cadence or form,
subtle variations on silence;

now that it is more timetable
than emotion, more arrival
than yearning, more performance
than savouring, more fact
than feeling, more a rough
and aged tree than the frail,
ecstatic beauty of a flower in bloom,
more embers than flames
(but not ashes),
neither pleasure nor pain,
not even peace, simply
the practice of presence;

now that I feel most helpless,
most impotent, least on fire,
my love most wrinkled and bent;
now that at last, like
rising from deep slumber,
I begin to need you,
the stirring of beginning,
begin to want you in the arid
desert of my not wanting;
if this is love, while giving
still so little, then now,
perhaps, I begin to love.

Epilogue

Straw

He chased after words, sculpted, so he thought,
Language into light, insight, sense, feeling.
Withered his hand and mind, yet still he sought
Something divine, just a glimpse revealing
The mystery, not tearing but teasing
Open, a peep, a tiny pulling back
Of heaven's dense cloud, massaging, easing
Out some meaning, the sniffed scent of its track.
A poor man, not even a prophet's son,
Deaf, no *bene scripsisti* did he hear.
When all was written, spoken, and all done,
Everything then finally became clear.
No vision was needed, with lesser lights he saw,
In that glorious flame and shine his work was straw.

Index of first lines

A tent-peg through your temple	26
As He fell, so it all falls apart	33
Before me a Ford Fiesta	18
Between the wild air and the turf, the dragon roars	10
Buttons are too binding	62
Chattering and clattering cups	10
Crisp. Crunchy	45
Every tree is a poem	4
Flower, you poke your fragile head up through the soil	47
Geese-plopped, pond-side poo	7
He chased after words, sculpted, so he thought	71
He comes into view	51
He hangs, *Opus Dei*	34
Here in this bright greyness, in this mild chill	44
Here in this city, what future for God?	15
How cruel, star, to be subject to our will	30
I am clay, dust	23
I am here, in winter 15/16	1
I can only hope. It is the ferry	40
I cannot be subtle	55
I have nothing to say, and you likewise	43
I lie here, Spirit, awaiting your fire	29
I pray, you block, like a cricketer	68
Inside your Cross, your wounds, inside	49
Like an ugly wife but with other charms	21
Like small children watching other boys' games	20
Listen, Lord, your client is complaining	27
Lost, like a trapped animal	66
My chocolate clock is melting	65
Not everything we see can be written down	39

Index of first lines

Not only their colour and shade, leaves	5
Now that I can't talk to you	69
One word	36
Perfume of the night; fragrance of the rose	4
Spirit, you are the fire, the igniter	59
Tame flame signalling silence in peaceful prayer	64
The Cross that I bear badly but I bear	58
The field stretches before me, its restful	57
The fighting boy…	25
The monstrance glass like a diver's mask	46
There is a yes which is no and a no which is yes	31
This cagèd bird, crumb pecking	65
This wall I cannot climb, or so it seems	60
Water like a tomb, stone-closed	35
We have everything under control	61
We must connect, overcome the distance	8
With the first sun, when the tourists come out	11
Words slide across meaning	38
Would I woo you with words	64
You are not talking, your silence	43
Your silence	53
Your triple kiss, a first	19
Your word is silence, wrapped in pain's darkness	61

SLG PRESS PUBLICATIONS

FP1	*Prayer and the Life of Reconciliation*	Gilbert Shaw (1969)
FP2	*Aloneness not Loneliness*	Mother Mary Clare SLG (1969)
FP4	*Intercession*	Mother Mary Clare SLG (1969)
FP8	*Prayer: Extracts from the Teaching of Father Gilbert Shaw*	Gilbert Shaw (1973)
FP12	*Learning to Pray*	Mother Mary Clare SLG (1970)
FP15	*Death, the Gateway to Life*	Gilbert Shaw (1971, 3/2024)
FP16	*The Victory of the Cross*	Dumitru Stăniloae (1970, 3/2023)
FP26	*The Message of Saint Seraphim*	Irina Gorainov (1974)
FP28	*Julian of Norwich: Four Studies to Commemorate the Sixth Centenary of the Revelations of Divine Love*	Sister Benedicta Ward SLG, Sister Eileen Mary SLG, Sister Mary Paul SLG, A. M. Allchin (1973, 3/2022)
FP43	*The Power of the Name: The Jesus Prayer in Orthodox Spirituality*	Kallistos Ware (1974)
FP46	*Prayer and Contemplation* and *Distractions are for Healing*	Robert Llewelyn (1975, 2/2024)
FP48	*The Wisdom of the Desert Fathers*	trans. Sister Benedicta Ward SLG (1975)
FP50	*Letters of Saint Antony the Great*	trans. Derwas Chitty (1975, 2/2021)
FP54	*From Loneliness to Solitude*	Roland Walls (1976)
FP55	*Theology and Spirituality*	Andrew Louth (1976, rev. 1978, 3/2024)
FP61	*Kabir: The Way of Love and Paradox*	Sister Rosemary SLG (1977)
FP62	*Anselm of Canterbury: A Monastic Scholar*	Sister Benedicta Ward SLG (1973, 2/2024)
FP67	*Mary and the Mystery of the Incarnation: An Essay on the Mother of God in the Theology of Karl Barth*	Andrew Louth (1977, 2/2024)
FP68	*Trinity and Incarnation in Anglican Tradition*	A. M. Allchin (1977, 2/2024)
FP70	*Facing Depression*	Gonville ffrench-Beytagh (1978, 2/2020)
FP71	*The Single Person*	Philip Welsh (1979)
FP72	*The Letters of Ammonas, Successor of St Antony*	trans. Derwas Chitty, introd. Sebastian Brock (1979, 2/2023)
FP74	*George Herbert, Priest and Poet*	Kenneth Mason (1980)
FP75	*A Study of Wisdom: Three Tracts by the Author of The Cloud of Unknowing*	trans. Clifton Wolters (1980)
FP81	*The Psalms: Prayer Book of the Bible*	Dietrich Bonhoeffer, trans. Sister Isabel SLG (1982, rev. 3/2025)
FP82	*Prayer & Holiness: The Icon of Man Renewed in God*	Dumitru Stăniloae (1982, rev. 2/2023)
FP85	*Walter Hilton: Eight Chapters on Perfection & Angels' Song*	trans. Rosemary Dorward (1983, rev. 3/2024)
FP88	*Creative Suffering*	Iulia de Beausobre (1989)
FP90	*Bringing Forth Christ: Five Feasts of the Child Jesus by St Bonaventure*	trans. Eric Doyle OFM (1984, 3/2024)
FP92	*Gentleness in John of the Cross*	Thomas Kane (1985)
FP94	*Saint Gregory Nazianzen: Selected Poems*	trans. John McGuckin (1986, 2/2024)

FP95	*The World of the Desert Fathers: Stories and Sayings from the Anonymous Series of the Apophthegmata Patrum*	trans. Columba Stewart OSB (1986, 2/2020)
FP104	*Growing Old with God*	Timothy N. Rudd (1988, 2/2020)
FP106	*Julian Reconsidered*	Kenneth Leech, Sister Benedicta Ward SLG (1988/ rev. 2/2024)
FP108	*The Unicorn: Meditations on the Love of God*	Harry Galbraith Miller (1989)
FP109	*The Creativity of Diminishment*	Sister Anke (1990)
FP110	*Called to be Priests*	Hugh Wybrew (1989, updated 2/2024)
FP111	*A Kind of Watershed: An Anglican Lay View of Sacramental Confession*	Christine North (1990, updated 2/2022)
FP116	*Jesus, the Living Lord*	Bishop Michael Ramsey (1992)
FP120	*The Monastic Letters of Saint Athanasius the Great*	trans. and introd. Leslie Barnard (1994, 2/2023)
FP122	*The Hidden Joy*	Sister Jane SLG, ed. Dorothy Sutherland (1994)
FP124	*Prayer of the Heart: An Approach to Silent Prayer and Prayer in the Night*	Alexander Ryrie (1995, 3/2020)
FP126	*Evelyn Underhill, Anglican Mystic: Two Centenary Essays*	A. M. Allchin, Bishop Michael Ramsey (1977, rev. 4/2025)
FP127	*Apostolate and the Mirrors of Paradox*	Sydney Evans, ed. Andrew Linzey & Brian Horne (1996)
FP128	*The Wisdom of Saint Isaac the Syrian*	Sebastian Brock (1997)
FP129	*Saint Thérèse of Lisieux: Her Relevance for Today*	Sister Eileen Mary SLG (1997)
FP130	*Expectations: Five Addresses for Those Beginning Ministry*	Sister Edmée SLG (1997, 2/2024)
FP131	*Scenes from Animal Life: Fables for the Enneagram Types*	Waltraud Kirschke, trans. Sister Isabel SLG (1998)
FP132	*Praying the Word of God: The Use of Lectio Divina*	Charles Dumont OCSO (1999)
FP133	*Love Unknown: Meditations on the Death and Resurrection of Jesus*	John Barton (1999, 2/2024)
FP134	*The Hidden Way of Love: Jean-Pierre de Caussade's Spirituality of Abandonment*	Barry Conaway (1999, 2/2025)
FP135	*Shepherd and Servant: The Spiritual Theology of Saint Dunstan*	Douglas Dales (2000)
FP137	*Pilgrimage of the Heart*	Sister Benedicta Ward SLG (2001)
FP138	*Mixed Life*	Walter Hilton, trans. Rosemary Dorward (2001, enlarged rev. 3/2024)
FP139	*In the Footsteps of the Lord: The Teaching of Abba Isaiah of Scetis*	John Chryssavgis, Luke Penkett (2001, 2/2023)
FP140	*A Great Joy: Reflections on the Meaning of Christmas*	Kenneth Mason (2001)
FP141	*Bede and the Psalter*	Sister Benedicta Ward SLG (2002, 2/2024)
FP142	*Abhishiktananda: A Memoir of Dom Henri Le Saux*	Murray Rogers, David Barton (2003)
FP143	*Friendship in God: The Encounter of Evelyn Underhill & Sorella Maria of Campello*	A. M. Allchin (2003, rev. 2/2025)
FP144	*Christian Imagination in Poetry and Polity: Some Anglican Voices from Temple to Herbert*	Bishop Rowan Williams (2004)
FP145	*The Reflections of Abba Zosimas: Monk of the Palestinian Desert*	trans. and introd. John Chryssavgis (2005, 3/2022)
FP146	*The Gift of Theology: The Trinitarian Vision of Ann Griffiths and Elizabeth of Dijon*	A. M. Allchin (2005)
FP147	*Sacrifice and Spirit*	Bishop Michael Ramsey (2005)
FP148	*Saint John Cassian on Prayer*	trans. A. M. Casiday (2006, 2/2024)
FP149	*Hymns of Saint Ephrem the Syrian*	trans. Mary Hansbury (2006, 2/2024)

FP150	*Suffering: Why All this Suffering? What Do I Do about It?*	
	Reinhard Körner OCD, trans. Sister Avis Mary SLG (2006)	
FP151	*A True Easter: The Synod of Whitby 664 AD*	Sister Benedicta Ward SLG (2007, 2/2023)
FP152	*Prayer as Self-Offering*	Alexander Ryrie (2007)
FP153	*From Perfection to the Elixir: How George Herbert Fashioned a Famous Poem*	
	Benedick de la Mare (2008, 2/2024)	
FP154	*The Jesus Prayer: Gospel Soundings*	Sister Pauline Margaret CHN (2008)
FP155	*Loving God Whatever: Through the Year with Sister Jane*	Sister Jane SLG (2006)
FP156	*Prayer and Meditation for a Sleepless Night*	
	SISTERS OF THE LOVE OF GOD (1993, 3/2024)	
FP157	*Being There: Caring for the Bereaved*	John Porter (2009)
FP158	*Learn to Be at Peace: The Practice of Stillness*	Andrew Norman (2010)
FP159	*From Holy Week to Easter*	George Pattison (2010)
FP160	*Strength in Weakness: The Scandal of the Cross*	John W. Rogerson (2010)
FP161	*Augustine Baker: Frontiers of the Spirit*	Victor de Waal (2010, 2/2025)
FP162	*Out of the Depths*	
	Gonville ffrench-Beytagh; epilogue Wendy Robinson (1990, 2/2010)	
FP163	*God and Darkness: A Carmelite Perspective*	
	Gemma Hinricher OCD, trans. Sister Avis Mary SLG (2010)	
FP164	*The Gift of Joy*	Curtis Almquist SSJE (2011)
FP165	*'I Have Called You Friends': Suggestions for the Spiritual Life Based on the Farewell Discourses of Jesus*	Reinhard Körner OCD (2012)
FP166	*Leisure*	Mother Mary Clare SLG (2012)
FP167	*Carmelite Ascent: An Introduction to Saint Teresa and Saint John of the Cross*	
	Mother Mary Clare SLG (1973, rev. 2/2012)	
FP168	*Ann Griffiths and Her Writings*	Llewellyn Cumings (2012)
FP169	*The Our Father*	Sister Benedicta Ward SLG (2012)
FP171	*The Spiritual Wisdom of the Syriac Book of Steps*	Robert A. Kitchen (2013)
FP172	*The Prayer of Silence*	Alexander Ryrie (2012)
FP173	*On Tour in Byzantium: Excerpts from The Spiritual Meadow of John Moschus*	
	Ralph Martin SSM (2013)	
FP174	*Monastic Life*	Bonnie Thurston (2016)
FP175	*Shall All Be Well? Reflections for Holy Week*	Graham Ward (2015)
FP176	*Solitude and Communion: Papers on the Hermit Life*	ed. A. M. Allchin (2015)
FP177	*The Prayers of Jacob of Serugh*	ed. Mary Hansbury (2015)
FP178	*The Monastic Hours of Prayer*	Sister Benedicta Ward SLG (2016)
FP179	*The Desert of the Heart: Daily Readings with the Desert Fathers*	
	trans. Sister Benedicta Ward SLG (2016)	
FP180	*In Company with Christ: Lent, Palm Sunday, Good Friday & Easter to Pentecost*	
	Sister Benedicta Ward SLG (2016)	
FP181	*Lazarus: Come Out! Reflections on John 11*	Bonnie Thurston (2017)
FP182	*Unknowing & Astonishment: Meditations on Faith for the Long Haul*	
	Christopher Scott (2018)	
FP183	*Pondering, Praying, Preaching: Romans 8*	Bonnie Thurston (2019, 2/2021)
FP184	*Shem`on the Graceful: Discourse on the Solitary Life*	
	trans. and introd. Mary Hansbury (2020)	
FP185	*God Under My Roof: Celtic Songs and Blessings*	Esther de Waal (2020)
FP186	*Journeying with the Jesus Prayer*	James F. Wellington (2020)

FP187	Poet of the Word: Re-reading Scripture with Ephraem the Syrian	
		Aelred Partridge OC (2020)
FP188	Identity and Ritual	Alan Griffiths (2021)
FP189	River of the Spirit: The Spirituality of Simon Barrington-Ward	Andy Lord (2021)
FP190	Prayer and the Struggle against Evil	John Barton, Daniel Lloyd, James Ramsay, Alexander Ryrie (2021)
FP191	Dante's Spiritual Journey: A Reading of the Divine Comedy	Tony Dickinson (2021)
FP192	Jesus the Undistorted Image of God	John Townroe (2022)
FP193	Our Deepest Desire: Prayer, Fasting & Almsgiving in the Writings of Saint Augustine of Hippo	Sister Susan SLG (2022)
FP194	Lent with George Herbert	Tony Dickinson (2022)
FP195	Four Ways to the Cross	Tony Dickinson (2022)
FP196	Anselm of Canterbury, Teacher of Prayer	Sister Benedicta Ward SLG (2022)
FP197	With One Heart and Mind: Prayers out of Stillness	Anthony Kemp (2023)
FP198	Sayings of the Urban Fathers & Mothers	James Ashdown (2023)
FP199	Doors	Sister Raphael SLG (2023)
FP200	Monastic Vocation SISTERS OF THE LOVE OF GOD, Bishop Rowan Williams (2021)	
FP201	An Ecology of the Heart: Faith Through the Climate Crisis	Duncan Forbes (2023)
FP202	'In the image of the Image': Gregory of Nyssa's Opposition to Slavery	Adam Couchman (2023)
FP203	Gregory of Nyssa and the Sins of Asia Minor	Jonathan Farrugia (2023)
FP204	Discovery	Arthur Bell (2023)
FP205	Living Healing: the Spirituality of Leanne Payne	Andy Lord (2023)
FP206	Still Listening: Sowing the Seeds of the Jesus Prayer	Bruce Batstone CJN (2023)
FP207	Julian of Norwich: Four Essays to Commemorate 650 Years of the Revelations of Divine Love Bishop Graham Usher, Father Colin CSWG, Sister Elizabeth Ruth Obbard OC, Mother Hilary Crupi OJN (2023)	
FP208	TIME	Dumitru Stăniloae, Kallistos Ware (2023)
FP209	Pearls of Life: A Lifebelt for the Spirit	Tony Dickinson (2024)
FP210	The Way and the Truth and the Life: An Exploration by a Follower of the Way	James Ramsay (2024)
FP211	Cosmos, Crisis & Christ: Essays of Wendy Robinson	Wendy Robinson (2024)
FP212	Towards a Theology of Psychotherapy: The Spirituality of Wendy Robinson	Andrew Louth (2024)
FP213	Immersed in God and the World: Living Priestly Ministry	Andy Lord (2024)
FP214	The Road to Emmaus: A Sculptor's Journey through Time	Rodney Munday (2024)
FP215	Prayer Too Deep for Words	Sister Edmée SLG (2024)
FP216	The Prayers of St Isaac of Nineveh	Sebastian Brock (2024)
FP217	Two Medieval English Saints: Cuthbert and Alban	Sister Benedicta Ward SLG (2024)
FP218	Encountering the Depths	Mother Mary Clare SLG (1981, rev. 3/2024)
FP219	Conflict and Concord Sister Susan SLG, Bishop Humphrey Southern, Bronwen Neil, Sister Rosemary SLG, Sister Clare-Louise SLG (2024)	
FP220	Divine Love in the Song of Songs	Sister Edmée SLG (2024)
FP221	Zeal for the Faith: An Introduction to Christian-Muslim Dialogue	Tony Dickinson (2024)
FP222	Bernard & Abelard	Sister Edmée SLG (2024)
FP223	Eliot's Transitions: T. S. Eliot's Search for Identity and the Society of the Sacred Mission at Kelham Hall	Vincent Strudwick (2024)
FP224	Landscape, Soul and Spirit: Ecology, Prayer and Robert Macfarlane	Andy Lord (2025)

CONTEMPLATIVE POETRY SERIES

CP1	*Amado Nervo: Poems of Faith and Doubt*	trans. John Gallas (2021)
CP2	*Anglo-Saxon Poets: The High Roof of Heaven*	trans. John Gallas (2021)
CP3	*Middle English Poets: Where Grace Grows Ever Green*	ed. John Gallas (2021)
CP4	*The Voice inside Our Home: Selected Poems*	Edward Clarke (2022)
CP5	*Women & God: Drops in the Sea of Time*	trans. and ed. John Gallas (2022)
CP6	*Gabrielle de Coignard & Vittoria Colonna: Fly Not Too High*	trans. John Gallas (2022)
CP7	*Chancing on Sanctity: Selected Poems*	James Ramsay (2022)
CP8	*Gabriela Mistral: This Far Place*	trans. John Gallas (2023)
CP9	*Henry Vaughan & George Herbert: Divine Themes and Celestial Praise*	ed. Edward Clarke (2023)
CP10	*Love Will Come with Fire: Anthology*	SISTERS OF THE LOVE OF GOD (2023)
CP11	*Touchpapers: Anthology*	coll. and trans. John Gallas (2023)
CP12	*Seasons of my Soul: Selected Poems*	Clare McKerron (2023)
CP13	*Reinhard Sorge: Take Flight to God*	trans. John Gallas (2024)
CP14	*Embertide: Encountering Saint Frideswide*	Romola Parish (2024)
CP15	*Thomas Campion: Made All of Light*	ed. and introd. Julia Craig-McFeely (2024)
CP16	*When God Hides: Selected Poems*	Joseph Evans (2025)

VESTRY GUIDES

VG1	*The Visiting Minister: How to Welcome Visiting Clergy to Your Church*	Paul Monk (2021)
VG2	*Help! No Minister! or Please Take the Service*	Paul Monk (2022)
VG3	*The Liturgy of the Eucharist: An Introductory Guide*	Paul Monk (2024)

www.slgpress.co.uk

The Sisters of the Love of God is an Anglican community of women religious living a contemplative monastic life.

To learn more about the Community and the Convent of the Incarnation at Fairacres, Oxford, see our website www.slg.org.uk.

As well as supporting those seeking to follow a vocation to the monastic life, the Community has a number of forms of association for those who feel drawn to share in the Sisters' life of prayer:
Fellowship of the Love of God, Companions,
Priests Associate or Oblate Sisters.

For more information email sisters@slg.org.uk or write to
The Reverend Mother, Convent of the Incarnation, Parker Street,
Oxford, OX4 1TB, UK.